CONTENTS

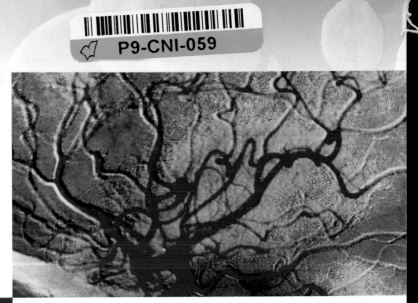

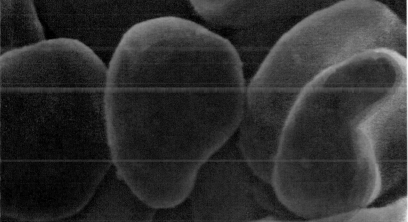

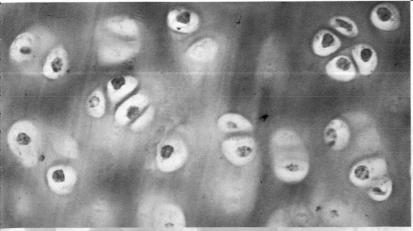

The brain's squishy tissue almost fills the skull

Filled with blood and air, the lungs appear dark purple

A JOURNEY INSIDE THE BODY

Medical scanners let doctors peer inside the body without even touching the skin. Scanners can make images of the insides of a living person's body, colour enhanced to highlight different features. This incredible image is a vertical slice through a nine-year-old boy, made by a machine called an MRI scanner. X-rays can show only hard tissue such as bone, but MRIs reveal soft tissue like the brain as well.

Trabecula, or strut, of bone

YOUR BODY

THE HUMAN BODY is more fascinating and complex than any machine ever invented. It is made up of microscopic units called cells, each containing its own set of complex instructions in the form of DNA. Cells of similar type are grouped together to form tissue, such as skin, blood, or bone. In turn, tissue forms larger structures called organs, such as the heart or brain. Until the recent past, it was possible for scientists to observe the inner workings of only dead or diseased bodies, during operations or postmortem examinations. Today, with the latest scanners, microscopes, and cameras, we can see healthy living organs and tissues at work, and zoom in on the tiniest cells with amazing clarity.

Each hand contains 27 bones

The knee is a joint – a point where two or more bones meet

Powerful muscles, attached to the body's bones, make them move

The foot is a complex lever, hinged at the ankle

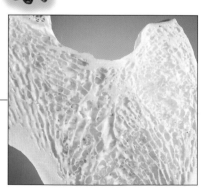

INSIDE A THIGH BONE

Your bones are made up of two main types of tissue. The outer part of bones is made of a dense, heavy tissue called compact bone, which gives bones their strength. Inside is spongy bone, which is filled with spaces to make bones lighter.

INSIDE COMPACT BONE

Like any other part of the body, compact bone is made of complex living tissue. It is constructed from microscopic cylinders called osteons. At the center of each osteon is a cavity containing tiny blood vessels. These supply bone cells with nutrients.

INSIDE SPONGY BONE

With an electron microscope, we can zoom in on a lattice of struts, or trabeculae, running through spongy bone. Even these solid connections are alive – embedded throughout them are microscopic cells that lay down minerals to strengthen the bone. In some bones, the spaces between the struts are filled with bone marrow, a type of tissue that makes blood cells.

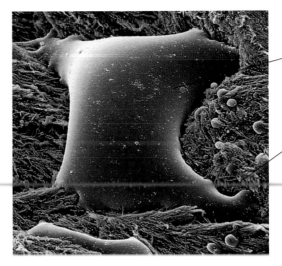

Main body of cell

Dissolving minerals around bone cell

BONE CELL

All the body's tissues are made of individual units called cells. This is one type of bone cell, an osteoclast, magnified more than 300 times. Its job is to dissolve bone to release minerals into the blood. Other types of bone cell do the opposite job, turning minerals into bone. Like many other types of tissue, bone is continually being broken down and rebuilt as we grow and age.

CHROMOSOMES

The control center of a cell is its nucleus. Packed into the nucleus are 23 pairs of chromosomes, one of each pair from your mother and one from your father. These carry your genes, encoded in a molecule called DNA.

A chromosome is made up of tightly coiled DNA

DNA spiral

THE STUFF OF LIFE

The DNA molecule is shaped like a twisted ladder – a shape known as a double helix. At the ends of the ladder's rungs are chemical units called bases, shown by colored blobs in this computer model. The sequence of these groups forms a chemical code – your DNA sequence. This code contains all the genes needed to make a human being.

Link between base pairs

Model of DNA molecule

IN YOUR HEAD

YOUR HEAD IS HOME to your body's control center: the brain. A delicate organ, the brain lies wrapped in layers of protective tissue and bone. It is encased by a triple layer of membranes and a special cushioning fluid. Surrounding the membranes is the skull. This solid case of bone acts like armor plating to safeguard its precious contents. The skull is covered by a flexible jacket of skin, muscle, and fat, which is nourished by blood vessels. This is your scalp. Hair growing out of the scalp keeps your head warm by trapping air close to the skin. Your head also contains the most important of the sense organs – eyes, ears, nose, mouth, and tongue – located close to the brain to aid direct communication.

3

EXPLORING YOUR HEAD

1 **Scalp:** *layer of skin and outer tissue of head including fat and muscle*

2 **Cranium:** *8 curved bones fixed together enclose the brain*

3 **Suture:** *fixed joint between bones of the skull*

4 **Meninges:** *3 layered protective membranes surround the brain*

5 **White matter:** *mostly nerve fibers (axons) that carry information*

6 **Gray matter:** *very closely packed nerve cells*

7 **Gyri and sulci:** *folds and creases allow for maximum surface area*

8 **Cavernus sinus:** *large vein that runs over the top of the brain*

9 **Ventricle:** *space within the brain filled with protective fluid*

10 **Optic nerve:** *carries visual information from the eye to the brain*

11 **Bony orbit:** *wall of orbital cavity, made of bone to protect the eye*

12 **Eyeball:** *sits within bony orbit and is attached to optic nerve*

BONE STRUCTURE

The skull is composed of curved, platelike bones that fit together tightly like pieces in a jigsaw puzzle. The bones in other parts of the skeleton are joined loosely so that they can move around. An outer covering of dense, compact bone and an inner layer of lighter, spongy bone make bones both strong and light.

Compact bone

Shoulder joint

Spongy bone

Listening

Speaking

In conversation

Back of brain

WATCHING THE BRAIN

Brain scanners can show which parts of the brain are busiest at any moment. These three scans show different areas lighting up during a conversation. When listening, the part of the brain that receives data from the ears is activated. When speaking, the area that tells the vocal cords to make sounds comes alive. In conversation, several areas of the brain are involved.

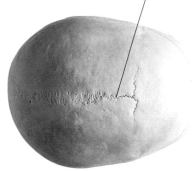

Suture, *showing where the bones of the skull have fused*

Anterior fontanelle

HARD HEADED

The cranium, the part of the head that surrounds the brain, is made of eight different bones fitted tightly together. But they don't join together until about 18 months of age. Before that, they're separated by membrane-filled gaps called fontanelles. These gaps enable the skull to be squeezed during birth, making the baby less likely to get stuck in the birth canal. Also, they allow for rapid brain growth during infancy.

BRAIN POWER

THE BRAIN IS THE MOST AMAZING organ in the human body and the most mysterious. Somehow, this cauliflower-sized mass of gray sludge creates your whole inner world. Everything you see, touch, think, dream, and remember is generated within it. The brain seems to work like an incredibly complicated computer – but one that is continually rewiring itself as it learns and adapts. Its basic component is the neuron – a spindly, wirelike cell that works by sending electrical signals to other neurons. There are more than 100 billion neurons in the brain, and each has up to 100,000 connections. Every second, trillions of electrical signals dart among our neurons at speeds of up to 250 mph (400 kph), weaving infinitely tangled paths through the maze of connections.

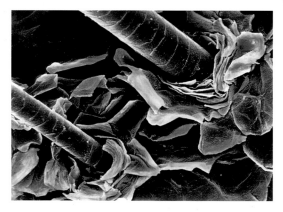

HAIRY HAT

Your scalp is dotted with about 10,000 tiny openings called follicles. A single hair grows from each one. The hair on your head is not just for decoration – it acts like an all-weather hat. It stops heat from escaping from your head and, when the weather is hot, it protects your scalp from sunburn.

A SLICE OF THE HEAD

An MRI scanner has created this image of a slice through the head. It clearly shows how the brain is constructed of different sections. Each of these sections has a different, specific function. The main part of the brain, the wrinkly cerebrum, is itself divided into two connected hemispheres, which have different abilities. The left side is usually best at math and language, while the right is better at visual skills, such as recognizing faces.

Cerebrum, where thought processes, memory, and conscious movement are processed

Corpus callosum, the bridge between the two sides of the brain

Cerebellum coordinates movement and balance

Brain stem regulates vital functions such as breathing

Spinal cord connects the brain with the rest of the body

Axon

Cell body

Dendrites

NETWORK OF NERVES

Each neuron, or nerve cell, has one axon that carries away outgoing signals, and up to 100,000 branching dendrites that carry incoming signals to the cell body. The connections between neurons are not fixed. As you grow and learn, new connections form and old ones become strengthened. But, when you age, dendrites wither away and the number of connections falls.

A dense mass of blood vessels ensures each brain cell is supplied with energy

Carotid artery supplies blood to head

FEEDING THE BRAIN

The brain is a hungry organ and, although relatively small, it takes a fifth of all the blood pumped by the heart. The blood delivers the vital oxygen and sugar that neurons need to keep generating electrical signals. If the blood supply to the brain stops for more than a few minutes, brain cells begin to die.

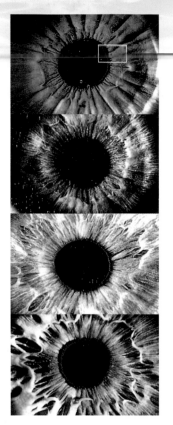

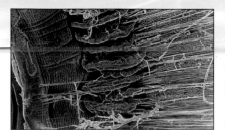

INSIDE THE IRIS

The iris is made of two muscles. One is circular and the other radial, like the spokes on a bike wheel. These muscles control the size of the pupil – the black hole that lets light enter the eye. They work to protect the retina from bright light and to maximize the ability to see in the dark.

Light enters the retina through these ganglion cells

EYES AND EARS

EYES AND EARS are the body's most important sense organs, keeping you constantly aware of the world around you. They work by taking in information about the world and converting it into a stream of electrical signals that the brain can understand. Because humans have two eyes and two ears, everything is seen and heard twice. The brain pools all the sensory information to provide stereo hearing and 3D vision. As well as sensing sound, ears monitor the posture and movement of the body, helping you balance.

Rods and cones are in this area

EYE COLOR

Irises – the colored part of eyes – are as unique as fingerprints. Everyone has a different color and pattern. But all the variations in eye color are produced by differing amounts of just one pigment – melanin, the same substance that determines skin color.

Optic nerve takes visual information to brain

Retina is deep inside the eyeball

Eyeball is filled with transparent jelly that lets light pass through

LIGHT AND COLOR

Your retinas contain two types of light-sensitive cells: rods and cones. Cones are good at detecting color, but they need bright light to work well. Rods work best in dim light, but they can't detect color. At night you see mainly with your rod cells, which is why you can't distinguish colors in dim light.

OPERATING THE EYE

The human eye works much like a camera. The eye's lens works in the same way as a camera's telephoto lens – changing shape to focus on near or distant objects. At the back of the eye is a light-sensitive surface called the retina. Together, the cornea (the eye's surface) and lens focus light onto the retina to produce an image, just as a camera focuses light onto a strip of film.

Lens becomes thinner or thicker to vary focus

THE EAR

The flaps of skin that we call ears are just the visible part of this sense organ. They collect air vibrations and funnel them to the eardrum, where the vibrations are magnified. In the inner ear, deep inside the skull, the vibrations are turned into electrical impulses and sent to the brain.

Sound consists of vibrations in the air

Auditory canal leads to eardrum

Cochlea is a long, coiled tube, filled with fluid, inside the inner ear

Auditory nerve takes messages to brain

Eustachian tube connects the ear to the back of the throat

DRUM SET

This membrane is the eardrum. It is so delicate that it vibrates as the sound waves hit it. Joined to the other side of the eardrum are three minute bones. Hinged together like a tiny machine, they magnify the vibrations and transfer them to the inner ear.

These three tiny bones, called auditory ossicles, sit behind the eardrum

WELL-BALANCED

Inside the inner ear is a set of three fluid-filled tubes called semicircular canals. Whenever you move, fluid moves inside at least one of these canals. Receptor cells at the ends of the canals detect this movement and send signals to the brain, helping you to keep your balance.

Cornea is clear and curved

Iris

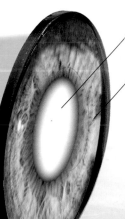

WIRED FOR SOUND

These hair cells are located in a membrane inside the cochlea. The inner ear is filled with fluid, which ripples when sound vibrations pass through it. These ripples make the membrane vibrate. The tiny hairs are disturbed by the vibrations, which makes them generate electrical signals that travel to the brain. Here, they are interpreted as sound.

Area sensitive
to bitter
flavors

Sour tastes
register here

THE TONGUE AND TASTE

Although food comes in an infinite
variety of flavors, your tongue's
tastebuds recognize only four basic
tastes: salty, bitter, sour, and sweet.
Each is detected by a specific area of
the tongue. However, the flavor of food is
not just a matter of taste – it involves
smell, texture, and temperature as well.

Area sensitive
to salty flavors

The tip of the tongue
detects sweetness

NOSE AND MOUTH

Y OUR NOSE AND MOUTH are miracles of
engineering, able to carry out an amazing
range of tasks simultaneously. Without them, you
would not be able to breathe, eat, smell, taste,
talk, or smile. Receptor cells in the mouth and
nose work together to examine food – anything
that smells or tastes unpleasant may not be safe.
Anything edible is mashed into a pulp by the
teeth, jaws, and tongue. Your nose and mouth are
also the entry point for the respiratory system,
taking in air destined for the lungs, and cleaning it
as you inhale. When you exhale, they help shape
the sound produced by the vocal cords, creating
one of the body's most incredible abilities: speech.

VERSATILE TONGUE

To grip food, the surface of
the tongue is covered with
hundreds of tiny bumps
called papillae, which give
it a rough texture. The
tongue and the lips work
together to modify sounds
from the vocal cords.

Large papilla

Small papillae contain
touch receptors

TASTE SENSATION

The tongue's papillae vary
in size. In crevices around
the largest papillae are taste
buds – clusters of chemical-
detecting cells. They
identify the substances that
make things sweet, bitter,
salty, or sour. When
triggered, they send
nerve signals zooming
to the brain to create
the experience of taste.

BABY TEETH

A baby's mouth is too small to house adult teeth, so the human body produces a set of just 20 smaller teeth, appearing from about six months of age. Designed to last the childhood years, they are eventually replaced by a set of 32 bigger, more firmly rooted adult teeth.

Enamel protects your tooth from wear and tear

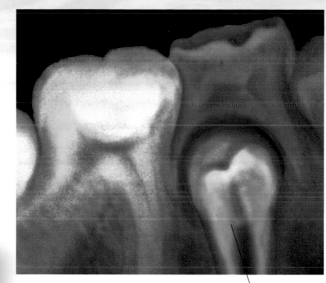

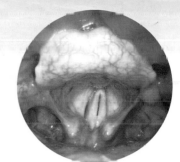

Closed vocal cords from above

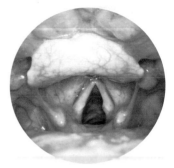

Open vocal cords allow air through

Adult tooth pushing out baby tooth

INSIDE A TOOTH

The hardest substance in the body is enamel – the white part of teeth. It is so tough that dentists need diamond-tipped drills to cut into it. Beneath the enamel is a slightly softer substance called dentine, and within this is the pulp cavity. This is the most sensitive area of a tooth, containing nerves and blood vessels. Your teeth also have roots that anchor them firmly in the jawbone.

SOUNDING OFF

Your voice starts with your vocal cords – two flaps of tissue like tight rubber bands. The cords open and close to control the passage of air through them. This moving air makes the cords vibrate to produce sound. The tighter the vocal cords, the higher-pitched the sound they produce.

UP YOUR NOSE

This scan shows the inside of the nose. A wall called the septum divides the nose into the two cavities that each open at a nostril. The top of each nasal cavity contains smell receptor cells. There are about 10 million smell receptors in your nose, each of which can detect a range of different chemicals.

Pulp cavity contains nerves and blood vessels

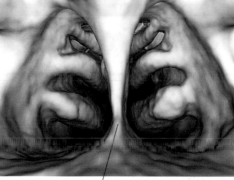

Septum

Root canal, hollow tube through which nerves and blood vessels pass

CLEAN SWEEP

The inside of the nose is covered with sticky mucus to trap flecks of dirt and germs. Minute hairs called cilia continually waft the mucus, with its cargo of dirt, toward the back of the throat to be swallowed. The acid in the stomach then kills the germs.

Root is buried in jawbone

Adult molar tooth

IN YOUR CHEST

T HE CHEST IS YOUR BODY'S POWERHOUSE. Its vital organs work nonstop to keep all the body's cells supplied with the blood and oxygen that keep them alive. In the center of your chest is the heart, a powerful, throbbing pump that drives blood throughout the body. Joining the top of the heart are the body's major blood vessels. The heart and blood vessels fit snugly in a space between the chest's other major organ: the lungs. These soft, spongelike structures almost completely fill the chest cavity. Surrounding the lungs is a two-layered, slippery membrane called the pleura and a protective cage of bones, the ribs.

4

EXPLORING YOUR CHEST

1 **Lungs *large*** *spongy organs for absorbing oxygen*

2 **Heart:** *powerful, muscular pump that drives the blood*

3 **Ribs:** *cage of bones, protects the organs inside the chest*

4 **Spine:** *tower of interlocking bones, supports the body*

5 **Oxygen-rich blood:** *traveling toward the arm and hand*

6 **Pulmonary blood vessels:** *carry blood through the lungs*

7 **Right atrium:** *collecting chamber of the heart, receives used blood*

8 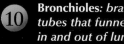 **Aortic arch:** *carries oxygen-rich blood away from the heart*

9 **Coronary artery:** *keeps the heart supplied with blood*

10 **Bronchioles:** *branching tubes that funnel air in and out of lungs*

PUMPING POWER

Every beat of your heart sends about half a cup of blood surging through your arteries. This X-ray shows the arch of the aorta, shaped like the handle of a cane, as it funnels blood from the heart. The aorta arches backward behind the heart, directing bloodflow toward the lower body.

— *Arch of aorta*

THE HEART

Right coronary artery, one of two major vessels that supply blood to the heart itself

Y OUR HEART IS A POWERFUL muscular pump that keeps blood flowing around your body. The amount of work it does is incredible. Even when you are resting, your heart is working harder than your leg muscles do when you are running – yet the heart never tires or stops for a rest. It beats about 70 times a minute, 100,000 times a day, and 40 million times a year. The heart is really a double pump. The left half sends oxygen-rich (fresh) blood all over the body, where some of the oxygen is used up by the body's cells. The right half sends the used blood to the lungs to pick up oxygen. The left half has the thicker muscle, as it has to pump at a higher pressure to reach the whole body.

HEARTBEAT

The heart is about the same size as a fist, but much stronger. When it beats, its muscular walls squeeze tighter than your fist can clench, forcing blood out of the large vessels at the top.

Aorta

Pulmonary artery takes blood to the lungs

Left atrium receives fresh blood from the lungs

Right atrium receives used blood from the main veins

CHAMBERS

The heart has four chambers: one top collecting chamber, or atrium, and one lower pumping chamber, or ventricle, on each side. Used blood enters the right atrium first, then the right ventricle. The blood is then pumped to the lungs. Once oxygenated, it enters the left atrium, then the left ventricle – the most powerful of the heart's chambers. It leaves the heart through the aorta.

Right ventricle pumps used blood

Left ventricle pumps fresh blood

HEART STRINGS

Between each atrium and ventricle is a valve – a set of flaps that lets the blood flow in one direction only. Tough cords, called heart strings, anchor the flaps to the inside of the heart, making sure that the valve does not blow inside out, like an umbrella in the wind.

Left coronary artery
divides into two

TIRELESS MUSCLE

The heart's walls are made of cardiac muscle – a type of muscle unlike any other in the body. It can contract endlessly without tiring. This view through a microscope shows the inside of a single cardiac muscle cell. The muscle cells contract in a carefully orchestrated sequence, responding to waves of electricity that sweep across the heart with each beat.

FEEDING THE HEART

The heart has its own blood supply, called the coronary system. This X-ray shows the coronary arteries and the mesh of fine blood vessels that run through the heart's muscular walls, delivering fuel and oxygen to the busy cardiac muscle cells. This extensive vessel network means that new connections can easily be formed if any of the minor vessels become blocked or damaged.

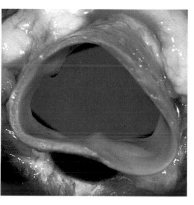

Heart valve open

Heart valve closed

ONE WAY ONLY

The rhythmic thump thump of a heartbeat is the sound of the valves snapping shut. These consist of flexible cup-shaped flaps. The valves are opened and closed by pressure changes in the blood on either side.

*Network of
arteries and veins*

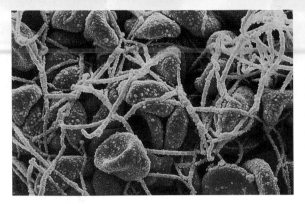

PLUGGING A LEAK

When you cut yourself, your body acts quickly. If the cut is small, clotting happens in just seconds. Tiny blood cells called platelets stick together in clumps to form a solid plug that blocks the hole. At the same time, a protein called fibrinogen forms a mesh of fibers that trap blood cells like fish in a net.

BLOODSTREAM

YOUR BLOODSTREAM IS a living transportation system. Driven by the heart, blood travels around the body continuously, delivering all the chemicals and oxygen that cells need, transporting special cells that help fight infection, and carrying away waste. Blood flows through a vast network of hollow tubes called blood vessels, which extend all over the body, ensuring that every single cell is serviced. Altogether you have about 60,000 miles (100,000 km) of blood vessels. Blood travels around them in an endless circle, and the bloodstream completes the round trip up to three times every minute.

Plasma makes up about 56% of blood

White blood cells and platelets make up just 4% of blood

Red blood cells account for about 40% of blood

THE PURPOSE OF PLASMA

Blood is the only organ in the body that's a fluid. It's made up of a soupy mixture of cells and liquid. Watery plasma, the liquid part, contains the proteins needed to make blood clot. It also transports nutrients and hormones to cells, and carries away waste.

SPAGHETTI JUNCTION

When blood leaves the heart, it spurts along large vessels called arteries, which have thick, stretchy walls to withstand the pumping action of the heart. The biggest artery, the aorta, is as wide as a garden hose. The arteries branch into smaller and smaller vessels, becoming as tangled as spaghetti. These tiny vessels are called capillaries, and are just a tenth the width of a human hair.

White blood cells bristle with chemicals that germs stick to

RED AND WHITE

A single drop of blood contains about 7,000 white blood cells and five million red blood cells. The function of red cells, like plasma, is transportation, while white cells are concerned with defense. The red cells, or erythrocytes, are packed with a chemical called hemoglobin that carries oxygen. White blood cells are the body's soldiers. There are several types, including neutrophils and monocytes, which hunt and engulf invading germs, and lymphocytes, which produce killer antibodies.

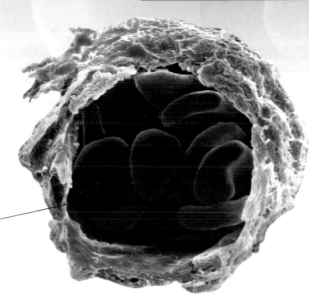

Doughnut-shaped, red blood cells have no nucleus, or core

Red blood cells can bend to move through tiny vessels

A TIGHT SQUEEZE

Some capillaries are so small that even red blood cells have to bend and squeeze through them. The capillaries' thin, flexible walls allow oxygen and food molecules to move from the blood cells to reach surrounding tissue cells.

Neutrophil, the most common white blood cell

Heart

Aorta, the biggest artery in the body

CIRCULATING BLOOD

Blood leaves the heart in arteries and travels in veins to get back to the heart. In most arteries the blood is bright red because it is full of oxygen. By the time it reaches the veins, it has used up some of the oxygen and turned dark red. This dark blood looks blue when seen through the walls of the veins. But blood is not really blue – even in royal families!

Veins are colored blue

Arteries are colored red

AIR PASSAGE
This view down a person's
windpipe shows where it branches
into two tubes (bronchi), one running
into each lung. The airways leading to
the lungs don't just carry air – they warm and
moisten it. Otherwise the delicate tissue inside the
lungs would dry out or get too cold to work properly.

*Rings of cartilage
stiffen the bronchi*

*Windpipe,
or trachea*

AIRWAYS

Y OUR LUNGS KEEP your body
continually supplied with the life-
giving gas oxygen, which comes from
fresh air. They work like large sponges,
except that they soak up air instead of
water. When you breathe in, your lungs
expand and suck air into a honeycomb
of tiny spaces. Your blood flows around
these air pockets, absorbing oxygen and
releasing the waste gas carbon dioxide,
which leaves the body when you breathe
out. Breathing is so important that you
don't have to try to do it. The brain
automatically monitors the amount of
oxygen and carbon dioxide in your blood
and adjusts your breathing to match.

*Cells under the cilia
secrete mucus*

BRONCHIAL TREE
Air enters the lungs
through a network of
hollow tubes arranged like an
upside-down tree. The trunk is
the windpipe. This runs down your
neck and into your chest, where it splits into branches
called bronchi. The bronchi run into the lungs,
dividing into smaller and smaller branches called
bronchioles, which lead into air pockets called alveoli.

SELF-CLEANING SYSTEM
The walls of the lungs secrete mucus to trap germs
and flecks of dust in the air. Tiny, hairlike strands
called cilia beat back and forth to drive the mucus
upwards, like an escalator. The mucus flows all
the way up to the throat, where it is swallowed.

ALVEOLI

You have about 600 million stretchy air pockets, or alveoli, in your lungs, each measuring a fraction of a millimeter across. Together they provide a vast surface area. This enables the lungs to inhale the maximum amount of oxygen and still fit comfortably inside the chest.

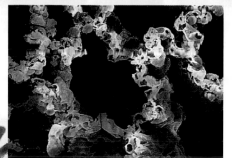

Air space within alveoli

BLOOD RUSH

This X-ray reveals the dense network of blood vessels leading from the heart (red) to the lungs. All the blood that flows from the right side of the heart goes directly to the lungs. After picking up oxygen, it goes straight back to the heart, where it is pumped by the left side to be shared between all the other organs.

Cast of the lung's airways

The tiniest bronchioles are finer than hairs

Pleura

SLIPPERY SURFACE

Enclosing the lungs is a double-layered membrane called the pleura. The two layers of the pleura have a tiny amount of fluid between them to help them slide easily over each other as you breathe in and out. The outer layer of the pleura is attached to the inside of the ribs. When the ribs move up, they stretch the lungs open and make them suck in air.

Cross-section through a person's lungs

IN YOUR ABDOMEN

THE SOFT, SQUISHY PART of your body between your chest and hips is called the abdomen. Many people use the word stomach to mean abdomen, but the stomach is only one of many organs packed cleverly together inside this part of the body. Most of these organs are soft and slippery, so a special folded membrane called the peritoneum holds them in place and supplies them with blood vessels. Outside the peritoneum is the wall of the abdomen – a flexible layer of muscle and skin. Most of the organs in the abdomen are involved in digesting food or keeping your blood clean and your body chemistry balanced. However, women's abdomens also contain their reproductive organs: ovaries, which make eggs, and the uterus, where babies develop.

4

EXPLORING YOUR ABDOMEN

1 **Liver:** *multifunctional organ, controls levels of many chemicals*

2 **Stomach:** *muscular bag that churns swallowed food and helps digest it*

3 **Colon:** *segmented tube, absorbs water from food waste*

4 **Omentum:** *apronlike fold of the peritoneum and fat*

5 **Ileum:** *longest part of the small intestine, absorbs food*

6 **Esophagus:** *tube carrying swallowed food to stomach*

7 **Adrenal gland:** *makes hormones including steroids and adrenaline*

8 **Chyme:** *soupy pool of partly digested food in stomach*

9 **Spleen:** *cleans blood by removing dead and aging cells*

10 **Kidney:** *one of a pair of organs that clean the blood*

11 **Vena cava:** *very large vein that carries blood back to the heart*

12 **Iliac artery:** *large artery that carries blood to the leg*

13 **Ureter:** *tube that carries wastes away from the kidney as urine*

14 **Bladder:** *stretchy chamber for storing urine until it leaves the body*

Larger blood
vessels are red

Glomeruli
are blue

BODY CHEMISTRY

Thousands of chemical reactions are taking place
in every cell in your body, all the time. This activity
keeps you alive, and it has to be continuously controlled
and monitored. A number of special organs take part in
this balancing act. The liver works like a chemical factory,
processing and storing useful substances and getting rid
of harmful ones. The kidneys control the amount of
water in the body, and dispose of some chemical
wastes. Other organs, such as the adrenal glands,
produce hormones. These chemical messengers
travel in the blood to target cells or tissues,
where they trigger specific changes,
sometimes affecting the way you feel.

TINY FILTERS

Inside each of the kidney's thousands of
filtering units, or nephrons, is a tiny knot of
blood vessels, called the glomerulus. It acts
as a microscopic sieve. As blood flows
through a glomerulus, water and small
molecules pass through the sieve into the
renal tubule. Useful chemicals are reabsorbed
from this tube, the rest sent to the bladder.

Cortex, outer part of
kidney, contains glomeruli

Medulla,
reabsorbs
water, making
urine more
concentrated

Renal
artery

Gall bladder, which
stores digestive bile

Spine

Rib

Scan through
the abdomen
showing the liver

Blood cells
flowing through
a lobule

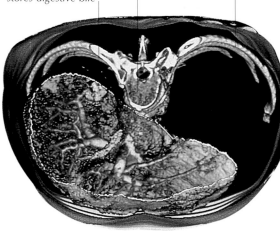

MULTITASK ORGAN

The liver is the heaviest
organ in the human body,
weighing about 3.5 lbs
(1.5 kg). It is made up of
thousands of small hexagonal
units called lobules, each of
which carries out hundreds of
different jobs. They break down
old blood cells and save their iron,
destroy poisons such as alcohol,
store vitamins and minerals,
and make digestive juices.

THE THRILL HORMONE

Whenever you feel frightened or excited, a hormone called adrenaline is at work in your body. Adrenaline comes from two small glands on top of the kidneys. Along with a related substance called noradrenaline, it has powerful effects all over the body, such as speeding up your heart and breathing, and increasing blood flow to your muscles. These effects make your body ready for action – the so-called fight or flight response. They also make dangerous sports like sky surfing all the more thrilling.

Renal pelvis, a funnel that collects urine and empties it into the bladder

Capsule, fibrous outer covering

Section of the small intestine, cutaway

Hormones are produced in clusters of special cells dotted all over the pancreas

The pancreas

SUGAR LEVEL

Behind the stomach and intestines is a long, slug-shaped organ – the pancreas. It has two main jobs: it secretes digestive enzymes into the small intestine, and it produces the hormones insulin and glucagen. These control the level of sugar in the blood. Sugar is one of the most important substances in the body – it is used as a fuel by all of your cells.

Insulin granule inside a pancreatic cell

Ureter, waterproof tube to bladder

A PAIR OF KIDNEYS

Your kidneys sit at the back of your abdomen. The right one is a bit lower down than the left because it's underneath the liver. The kidneys constantly clean the blood, filtering out harmful wastes and excess water, which then drain to the bladder as urine. Every day, about 440 gallons (1,700 liters) of blood is spring cleaned by the kidneys before rejoining the circulation.

27

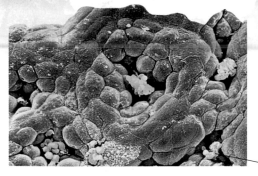

ACID BATH

As soon as you see or smell food, tiny glands in the wall of your stomach, like the one shown here, start secreting a liquid called gastric juice. Gastric juice contains the enzyme pepsin, which digests proteins in food like meat, eggs, and fish. It also contains a strong acid that activates pepsin and kills germs. Your stomach produces up to five pints (three liters) of gastric juice every day.

Food remnants inside the stomach

Colon (large intestine), shaped like three sides of a square, stretches around the edge of the abdomen

DIGESTION

DIGESTION IS THE PROCESS that turns the food you eat into simple chemicals your body can absorb. It takes 18–30 hours for a meal to complete its journey through the digestive tract. During this time the body uses a combination of mechanical and chemical weapons to reduce the food to its basic chemical constituents. Muscular spasms churn it around in the stomach and propel it along the small intestine's slippery tubes, while powerful enzymes and acid attack it chemically. Gradually the food fragments become smaller and smaller – until these are so tiny they can dissolve in blood. Waste material – mostly plant fiber and harmless bacteria – passes into the large intestine, or colon, and is eventually expelled from the body.

BLOOD SUPPLY

The digestive system receives a rich blood supply from two blood vessels called the mesenteric arteries. You can see blood traveling through the upper mesenteric artery in this X-ray. After a meal, extra blood is diverted through these arteries to help absorb the sudden flow of nutrients.

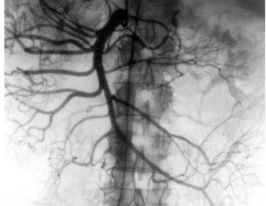

Appendix

ABSORBING FOOD

The surface of the small intestine has millions of tiny, fingerlike folds called villi. These are covered in even tinier folds called microvilli. This gives the intestine a huge surface area for absorbing digested food. The food molecules are drawn through the surface and enter the bloodstream.

Esophagus connects the throat to the stomach

Duodenum

Stomach is a J-shaped muscular bag

THE STOMACH

Your stomach works like a food processor: it churns the food around until it has turned from a lumpy mixture into a creamy liquid called chyme. The rugae let the stomach expand like a balloon so that it can hold even a five-course dinner.

Rugae (folds) lining the stomach wall

THE DUODENUM

The valve at the bottom of the stomach, called the pylorus, opens to let chyme squirt into the first part of the small intestine, called the duodenum. Here, the chyme mixes with powerful digestive juices from both the liver and the pancreas.

Pylorus, the exit from the stomach to the duodenum

THE SMALL INTESTINE

The walls of the small intestine have muscles that contract in waves to push food along. The shiny liquid coating the inner surface is mucus. It helps food slide and stops your digestive system from digesting itself – otherwise you would be eaten from the inside out.

Transverse (crosswise) folds in the small intestine

THE COLON

The way the muscles are arranged gives the colon a segmented appearance like an accordion – the segments constrict to squeeze the food along. Like a sponge, the colon sucks out any remaining water from the sludge.

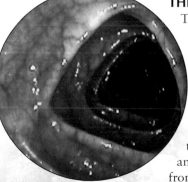

The colon, showing its segments from within

Small intestine measures about 20 feet (6 meters) in total

Rectum, a muscular chamber for storing feces before they are passed out of the body through the anus

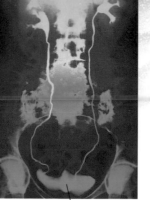

URINE STORE

At the bottom of the pelvic area is the bladder – a muscular, waterproof bag for storing urine. This X-ray shows urine in the bladder and the tubes that carried it from the kidneys. As the bladder stretches, receptor cells in its wall send signals to the brain, triggering the urge to go to the toilet.

Pool of dye-containing urine in the bladder

THE PELVIS

THE BONES YOU CAN FEEL jutting out at your hips are the sides of your pelvis – a large funnel-shaped basin of bone that supports the soft organs of the lower abdomen. Within this bowl are the intestines, the main waste-disposal organs (the bladder and rectum), and, in women, the reproductive organs. In pregnancy, the pelvis also becomes a cradle to hold and protect the growing baby. But the pelvis is not just for protection. It acts as a bridge between the spine and legs, and helps to distribute your weight evenly. Without a pelvis you would crumple into a heap, unable to stand or walk.

Shock-absorbing disks make the spine flexible

THE LOWER BACK

The individual bones of the spine – called vertebrae – are stacked together over the pelvis to form a sturdy column of bone, keeping the body upright. The spine ends with the sacrum – fused vertebrae that fit tightly into the back of the pelvis. The five lumbar vertebrae, those closest to the pelvis, carry most of the weight of the upper body, making the lower back susceptible to strain.

Bony projections are attachment sites for the muscles and ligaments that keep you upright

Base of spine attached to pelvis by two joints

CHILD SUPPORT

Normally, a woman's uterus, or womb, is the size of a small fist. But in pregnancy it can expand enormously, as shown in this X-ray of twins, taken 10 weeks before birth. The pelvis supports the extra weight and, when the mother gives birth, both babies will pass through it, one after the other. Women's pelvises are wider than men's to accommodate babies' large heads.

Upper twin lying horizontally

Head of lower twin is close to the base of the pelvis

Base of spine

Ilium, or hipbone

Sacrum

Coccyx, or tailbone

BASIN OF BONE

Your pelvis is made of six separate bones that fuse together as you grow. The bottom of the spine sits between two large flat bones. These are the ones you can feel – your hipbones. Their shape enables the muscles of the legs and torso to attach to them securely.

At the lower front on each side is the pubis bone, and above each pubis is a bone called the ischium. This is the bone that you sit on.

Head of thigh bone

Pubis

Ischium

Ovum is about 0.1mm wide

Round, flattened head

Long tail aids movement

A man's body produces about 300 million sperm every day

FEMALE SEX CELL

The pelvic area in women contains the uterus, ovaries, and fallopian tubes – the reproductive organs. About every 28 days, one of the two ovaries releases an ovum, or egg (the female sex cell), which travels down the tubes towards the uterus. If it meets a sperm cell, the two fuse together to form an embryo, which stays inside the uterus and grows into a baby.

MALE SEX CELLS

Men's bodies produce sex cells called sperm. Under a microscope they look like tadpoles, complete with wriggling tails. Sperm are made in bean-shaped organs called testes, which are in men's scrotums outside the warm abdominal cavity. This is because they need a low temperature to grow.

IN YOUR LEGS

WALKING SEEMS EFFORTLESS to us, yet it is so complicated that scientists are unable to replicate the activity in robots. Each of your legs is built around the two biggest bones in the body: the femur (thighbone) and the tibia (shinbone). Wrapped around these, and spanning the joints at their ends, are the body's most powerful muscles, arranged in complicated bundles. Whenever you take a stroll, the many bones and muscles in your hips, legs, and feet work together like instruments in an orchestra, moving in rhythmic sequence to carry your body forward.

The femur, or thighbone, is the longest bone in the body

Muscle fibers are made of very long thin cells arranged in parallel bundles

Tibia, the main bone of the shin

Quadriceps,
made up of four
different muscles

Leg muscles help
pump blood back
toward the heart
by squeezing
veins buried
deep inside them

The femur's
'knuckles' fit with
the tibia below to
form the knee,
the largest joint
in the body

The foot acts as
a lever when
you walk or run

EXPLORING YOUR LEGS

1 **Tendons:** *tough bands of connective tissue that attach muscles to bones*

2 **Calcaneus:** *heel bone, the main bone of the ankle joint*

3 **Knee:** *hinge joint where the femur and tibia meet each other*

4 **Synovial capsule:** *made of tough tissue, holds fluid to lubricate the joint*

5 **Muscle fibers:** *strandlike proteins slide over each other to make muscle contract*

6 **Bone marrow:** *soft tissue that stores fat or produces blood cells*

7 **Quadriceps:** *part of the muscle that straightens the knee*

8 **Spongy bone:** *honeycombed material in bones, contains the bone marrow*

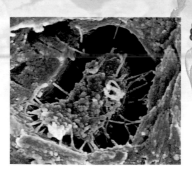

OSTEOCYTE

Deep inside even the hardest types of bone are spiderlike cells called osteocytes, nestling in tiny cavities. Osteocytes produce calcium and other minerals that make bones hard. Thin strands run from the osteocytes into the surrounding bone, carrying minerals and other chemicals that nourish and build the bone.

Fibula, or lesser shin bone

Phalanges, or toe bones

CIRCLES OF BONE

The minerals in bone are laid down in concentric circles like the rings in a tree trunk, an arrangement that gives great strength. Each set of rings is called an osteon and measures a fraction of an inch across. This cross section shows several osteons packed together. In the center of each is a hollow canal (black) through which blood vessels run. Around this are small cavities, each housing an osteocyte.

GROWING BONES

A newborn baby has more bones than an adult. This is because some bones meet and fuse together as a baby grows into a child. Many bones also get longer and wider. At each end of your leg and arm bones are growth-plates, where new bone is formed. This means that bones lengthen from both ends.

FRAMEWORK

Bones FORM THE SKELETON – the inner scaffolding that gives the body shape and allows you to move. Working together with the muscles that wrap around it, the skeleton acts like a complicated machine, allowing you to run at up to 15 miles (24 km) an hour, curl into a tight ball, or reach to scratch anywhere on your body. Bones make up about a quarter of your total body weight. Far from the dead, brittle objects we see in museums, bones are made of living tissue – they bleed when they are damaged and can mend themselves if broken. Weight for weight, your bones are stronger than iron or concrete.

LONG LEGS

Your legs have to carry your whole body weight, so they contain the longest and strongest bones – the femur and tibia. These are not solid and brittle, but hollow and very slightly flexible, making them both lightweight and strong. The bones of your feet form a flexible arch that can flatten and spring back into shape, acting as a shock-absorber.

The foot flattens as it takes the body's weight

MEETING POINTS

The skeleton would be useless if all the bones were fixed solidly to each other. Instead, they are held together loosely, forming a system of girders and levers that can move in relation to each other. The flexible meeting points between bones are called joints. Every part of your body that's bendable – like your hips, knees, and ankles – contains a joint.

Hip joint

Patella (kneecap) stops the knee from bending the wrong way

HINGE JOINT

The knee joint is enclosed and held together by the tough tissue of the synovial capsule. This in turn is wrapped in fibrous straps called ligaments. To keep the joint working smoothly, the bone ends are covered with a very smooth type of tissue called cartilage. The knee joint works like a hinge, allowing your lower leg to bend backward and forward.

Ligaments hold bones together

Femur, or thighbone, is the longest bone in the body

Cartilage forms a smooth surface on bone ends

Tibia, main shin bone

There are seven bones in each ankle

The big toe has only two bones; other toes have three

BONY FEET

More than half the total number of bones in the human body are in the hands and feet – each foot has 26 bones, and each hand has 27. Human foot bones have a similar arrangement to hand bones because we evolved from tree-dwelling apes who used their feet like hands to grasp branches. Today, we use our feet just for walking, but people without arms sometimes learn to pick up objects with their feet.

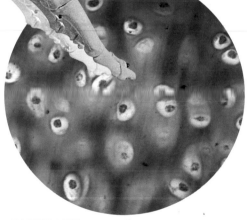

CARTILAGE

Cartilage is a very tough but smooth tissue that coats the ends of bones, helping joints to move easily. It consists of a tough network of fibers produced by cells called chondrocytes – the red and white blobs in this microscope view. As well as covering joints, cartilage forms your ears and the end of your nose.

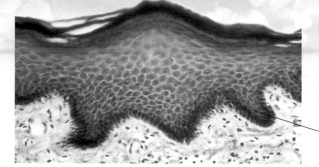

MELANIN

The cells that make the pigment melanin, which determines skin color, are in a layer just below the surface of the skin. Melanin spreads through the epidermis – the outer layer of the skin – giving a dark colour.

Melanocytes make the pigment melanin

BODY COVERING

SKIN IS THE BODY'S biggest sensory organ, packed with millions of nerve endings that respond to pressure, pain, heat, and cold. Without skin, you would be unable to touch the world around you. But skin is more than a sensory organ – it is also a protective armour, the body's first line of defense. If you had no skin to protect you, bacteria and other germs would quickly invade your body. Skin protects against many other dangers, too. It stops the internal organs from getting waterlogged, screens them from the sun's harmful rays, and helps prevent the body from overheating or freezing. It cushions the body against wear and tear. And, when it gets cut, skin has the amazing ability to mend itself, almost invisibly.

GOOSEBUMPS

When you get cold, tiny muscles pull the base of the hairs to make them stand on end. This traps body heat close to your skin, helping you to stay warm. The muscles also produce lumps under the hairs – goosebumps.

SKIN DEEP

Dark-skinned people have more melanin cells than fair-skinned people. Melanin helps protect you from the damaging effects of the sun's rays – that is why fair-skinned people get sunburned more easily.

Flattened, dead skin cells form the outer layer of the epidermis

Dermis contains nerves and blood vessels

The bottom layer of the epidermis continuously makes new cells

Flakes of skin
fall off your
body all the
time, forming
household dust

Sweat pore,
the opening of
a sweat gland

COOLING SWEAT

Scattered throughout your skin are about three million tiny
holes called sweat pores. When your body gets too warm, a
salty liquid – sweat – oozes out of these pores from glands deep
in the skin. As the sweat evaporates, it takes heat from the skin
and so helps cool the body down. You produce at least 0.3 liters
(0.5 pints) of sweat every day, even in cold weather.

HARD AS NAILS

Skin, hair, and nails all
get their strength from a
tough protein called
keratin. Nails are made of
flat plates of solid keratin
bonded together, as shown
here. Like the outermost
skin cells, nail cells are
dead, except in the root of
the nail where new cells
form. Fingernails grow
at the rate of about
2 in (5 cm) a year.
Toenails are less
than half as fast.

The soles of your
feet and the palms
of your hands are
the only areas of
skin with no hairs

THICK-SKINNED

Your skin is not the same
thickness throughout your body.
The thinnest skin, measuring just
0.02 in (0.5 mm) is on the eyelids. In
contrast, the skin on the soles of your
feet is at least 0.15 in (4 mm) thick.
Areas of skin can change their thickness
if they need to. If you walk barefoot a lot,
the soles of your feet will get even thicker.

Folds in the epidermis
give your skin ridges

SKIN LAYERS

The outer part of your skin, the epidermis, is continually replacing
itself. The cells in this layer keep dividing, pushing new cells upward.
As they travel up, the cells harden, flatten, and die, forming your skin's
tough outer barrier. When the cells reach the top, they break off in
flakes. Every day you shed about 50 million dead skin cells. Underneath
the epidermis is the dermis, a supple layer of cells laced with blood
vessels, pain and touch receptors, sweat glands, and the roots of hairs.

INDEX

ACKNOWLEDGMENTS

Dorling Kindersley would like to thank:
Chris Drew and Stefan Podhorodecki for modeling; Andy Crawford for photographing them; Beth Apple for editing the jacket text; Clare Lister for editorial assistance; Adrienne Hutchinson for design assistance; and Dorothy Frame for the index.

The publisher would like to thank the following for their kind permission to reproduce their photographs:
Key: a=above; b=below; c=center, l=left, r=right, t=top, ace=acetate;
Corbis: Richard Hutchings 14tl;
Denoyer - Geppert International: 12b, 13cr, 18cl, 18bc, 27cr; **Natural**

History Museum: 8ace cl; **The Image Bank/Getty Images:** Jump Run Productions 27tc; **Imagingbody.com:** 17cl; **Science Photo Library:** 6-7, 7cl, 7br, 19cr, 19crb, 19l, 23cr, 28c, 31tl; Michael Abbey 34bl; John Bavosi 35ca; Biology Media 33ace (br); BSIP, Gems Europe 23br, 26cl; BSIP VEM 15tc, 15br; John Burbridge 36tc; Dr Jeremy Burgess 37tl; CNRI 5tr, 11crb, 13c, 18tl, 27br, 29crb; Custom Medical Stock Photo 12b, 20-21; Prof C. Ferlaud/CNRI 15tr, 15cra; Martin Dohrn 24ace, 25, 36cra, Simon Fraser 4l, 8l; GJLP/CNRI 30l; A. Glauberman 9ace; Pascal Goetgheluck 15c, 22tl; Eric Grave 33 No.7; Mehau Kulyk

3c, 9l, 35bc; Mark Maio/King-Holmes 12tl; David M. Martin MD 29br; Juergen Berger, Max-Planck Institute 26-27t&b, 28-29t&b, 30-31t&b, 30-31b; Astrid & Hanns-Frieder Michler 6c; National Cancer Institute 3t & b, 4-5t&b, 18-19t&b, 20-21c, 20-21t&b, 22-23t&b, 38t & b; Susumu Nishinaga 20tl, 20bl, Endpapers; OMIKRON 14bl; Alfred Pasieka 7br, 10-11, 11tr, 13tr, 22 23, 26-27c, 28-29; Philippe Plailly 18br; Clinical Radiology Dept., Salisbury District Hospital 30tc, 31c; Motta & Familiari/Anatomy Dept/University La Sapienza, Rome 5cla, 5crb, 7t, 10bc, 13bc, 14cla, 21tr, 22bl, 23tc, 26bl, 28tl, 28bl, 31bl, 34tl; Quest 12tc, 12cra, 19tc, 26t, 34-35t&b, 36-37t&b, 36b; David Scharf 7cr; Dr Klaus Schiller 29tr, 29cra; Andrew Syred 6br, 7cl,

37cl; Tissuepix 14-15; Nancy Kedersha/UCLA 6-7t&b, 10-11t&b, 12-13t&b, 14-15t&b; Hugh Turvey 37tr; M. I. Walker 5bl, 35br; Wellcome Dept. of Cognitive Neurology 10tl; **The Wellcome Institute Library, London:** 13cl.

Jacket: Science Photo Library: Mehau Kulyk back tl; Omikron back tr.

All other images © Dorling Kindersley.
For further information see:
www.dkimages.com

Every effort has been made to trace copyright holders of photographs. The publishers apologize for any omissions.

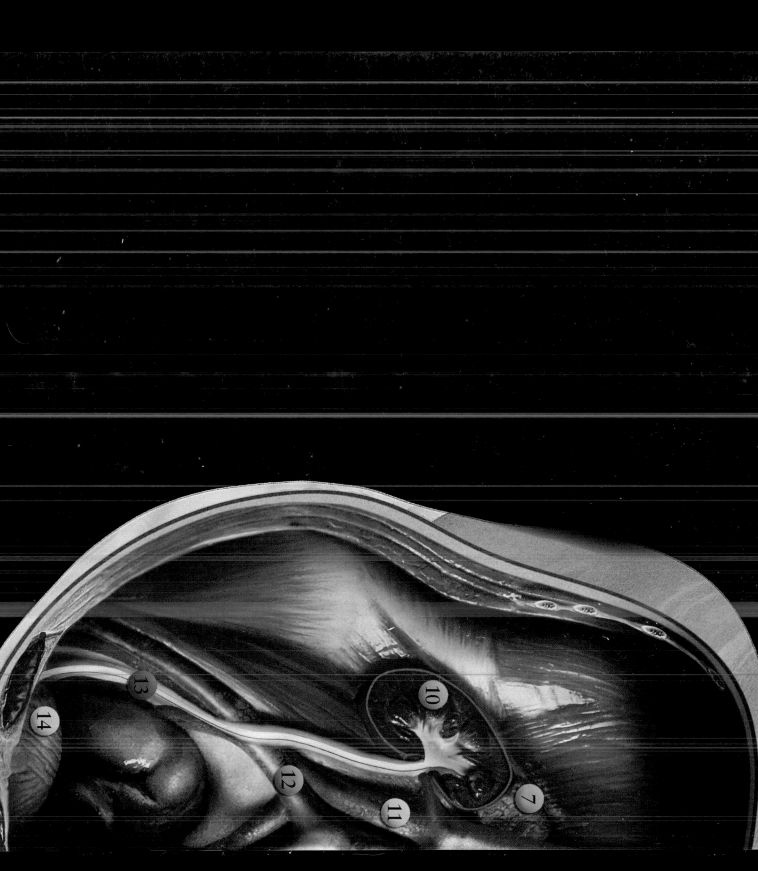

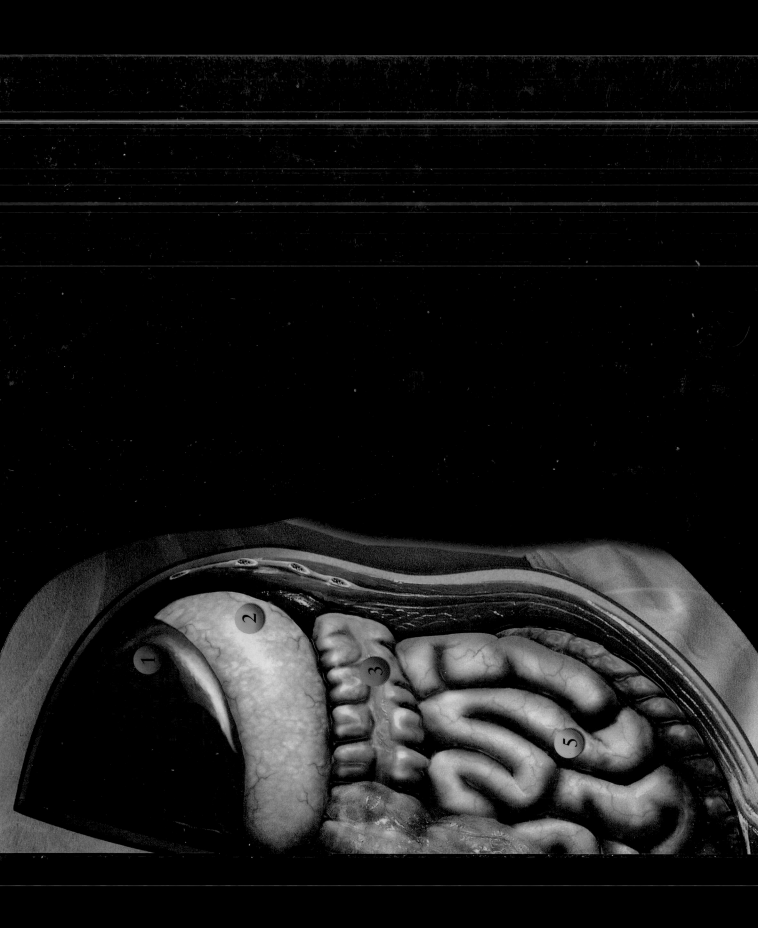

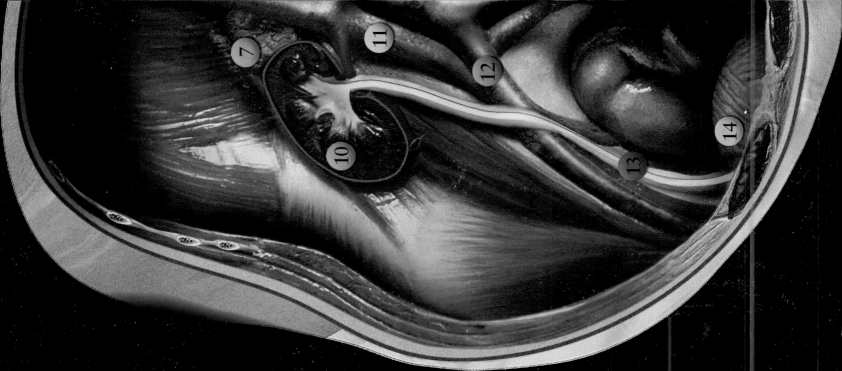